AF604679

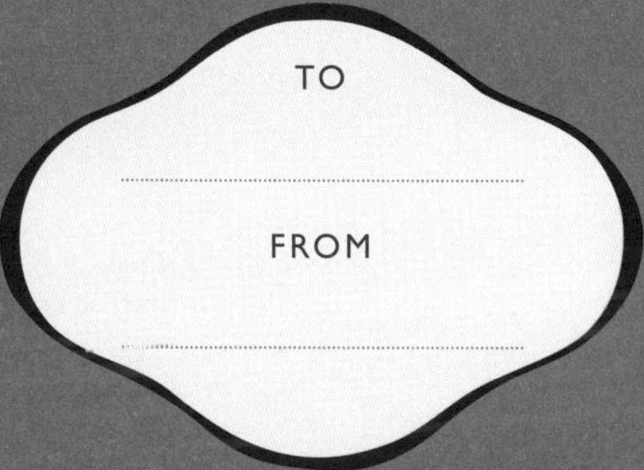
TO
FROM

A GUIDED KEEPSAKE JOURNAL

PENGUIN BOOKS

UK | USA | Canada | Ireland | Australia
India | New Zealand | South Africa | China

Penguin Books is part of the Penguin Random House group of companies
whose addresses can be found at global.penguinrandomhouse.com

First published by Penguin Books in 2025

Cover design by Adam Laszczuk © Penguin Random House Australia Pty Ltd
Internal design by Post Pre-Press Group, Australia
Typeset in Gill Sans by Post Pre-Press Group, Australia

Printed and bound in China by 1010 Printing International Limited

A catalogue record for this book is available from the National Library of Australia

ISBN 978 1 76135 326 0

penguin.com.au

We at Penguin Random House Australia acknowledge that Aboriginal and Torres Strait Islander peoples are the Traditional Custodians and the first storytellers of the lands on which we live and work. We honour Aboriginal and Torres Strait Islander peoples' continuous connection to Country, waters, skies and communities. We celebrate Aboriginal and Torres Strait Islander stories, traditions and living cultures; and we pay our respects to Elders past and present.

CONTENTS

CHILDHOOD

What is your earliest memory?

If you picture being a child, what sounds, smells and tastes come to mind?

Who did you spend the most time with as a child?

Did you have any pets growing up?
What were their names and what were they like?

What do you see when you think about your childhood home?

What were your wildest dreams when you were younger?
Did any of them come true?

Is there a particular object from your childhood that holds special meaning for you?

Where did your family typically spend a summer holiday?

Did you collect anything as a child?

What were your parents' personalities like?

How did you spend your time during school holidays?

Where did you go to primary school and what was it like?

Did you ever get into trouble at school or home? What happened?

How did you spend your time after school?

Which teacher had the most profound impact on you?

What were your favourite foods as a child?
Are there any things you loved to eat that aren't around today?

Is there an item of clothing from childhood
that had a special meaning for you?

What was your favourite book or story as a child?

What was your favourite film or TV show?

Did you have a favourite toy as a child?
What was it and did it have a special name?

What was the first sport you played and how did you rate your abilities?

What was a typical family meal like in your household?

Did you have any chores or responsibilities as a child? What were they?

What was the most memorable birthday party you had as a child?

Who was your first celebrity crush?

Who was your first non-celebrity crush?

What is a funny story from your childhood that you love to tell?

Who within your family did you look up to and want to be like when you were younger?

What were your favourite family traditions for Christmas or other holidays growing up?

If you had siblings, what were your relationships like? What were the causes of your typical disagreements?

Which parent were you closer to as a child?

Were you close with your cousins?
Do you have any fond memories of spending time with them?

TEENAGE YEARS

What five words would you use to describe your teenage years?

1.

2.

3.

4.

5.

What songs do you remember listening to the most?

What was your favourite meal or dish that your parents made?

What sports did you play during your teenage years?

What celebrities or famous people did you look up to and why?

What was the first car you drove and
what memories do you associate with it?

Where did you go to high school and what was your experience like?

What was your school formal like?

What do you remember from your last day of school?

What were some of your daily routines or rituals during high school?

How did you celebrate your 18th birthday?

Did you always know what you wanted to do after school?

Do you have any memories of sitting school exams?
What were they like for you?

What do you remember about the summer holidays after finishing school?

What was your first job, and what did you learn from it?

Did you have any difficult moments when you were
a teenager that shaped you into the person you are today?

How did your friendships change and evolve during your teenage years?

Are you still in touch with any close friends from your teenage years today?

What were some of your hobbies and how did they enrich your life?

When you were in your teens, was there a person you looked up to and wanted to be like?

Did you ever keep a diary or journal growing up, or document your memories in other ways?

What was the most rebellious thing you did as a teenager?

Was there a hangout spot where you and your friends loved to spend time?

How did you spend your weekends or free time as a teenager?

What was the first thing you saved up with your own money to buy?

How old were you when you learned to drive?
Who taught you? Did you pass your test the first time?

What would you tell your teenage self
if you could write him a letter now?

YOUNG ADULTHOOD

At the time you left school, was there a particular career you had in mind?

Did you move away from home for your career or to study?
Was it something you enjoyed?

How did you manage your finances when you first started earning money?

What was your first full-time job and how did you get it? Was it a good experience?

Did you participate in any significant events, like protests or movements?

Was there a concert, band, or cultural moment from this time that sticks out to you as important?

What sport team did you follow, and do you still follow them?

What event or wedding did you attend that was the most memorable during this time?

Who were the most important people in your life in your twenties, and are you still connected today?

Is there a decision you made in your twenties that changed the course of your life?

What was your biggest dream or goal in your twenties, and did you achieve it?

What were your main interests outside of work in your twenties?

What was a useful piece of advice somebody told you before you turned 30?

Was there a particular place that played a significant role in your young adulthood? What made it important?

How did you cope with stress and pressure in your young adulthood?

Did you experience any significant physical or mental challenges?
What helped you overcome them?

How did you cope with your first major break-up?

If you embarked on an overseas adventure how did it change the way you saw the world and yourself? Write down everywhere you travelled to that you can recall.

What do you consider to be the most reckless decision you made in young adulthood? How did it work out?

What memories make you most nostalgic for your twenties?

What were you most afraid of when you were becoming an adult, and did you work on overcoming this fear?

Did you ever have a significant friendship fall apart in your twenties? If so, what happened?

Describe the first person you said 'I love you' to – did it work out between you?

How did your relationship with your family change when you were a young adult?

What was your favourite memory from your 21st birthday?

What do you remember from your 30th birthday?

What achievements did your family or friends make that made you feel the proudest of them?

What did you most look forward to doing on the weekend?

What was your favourite city or place to regularly visit?

ADULTHOOD

What object holds the most significance to you?

What activity brings you the most joy?

What is your biggest fear?

What do you recall about the first home you bought?

If you're married, what do you remember most from your wedding day?

What was the most challenging part about growing up?

How did you make time for friends at this stage in life?

How did you manage work-life balance as a parent?

How did your dream job or profession evolve over time?

Outside of work and family, what other activities or hobbies did you regularly do?

What was your biggest financial challenge, and what steps did you take to overcome it?

What memories stick out to you when you think about your early days of parenthood?

How did you choose your children's names?

What family holidays hold the best memories?

How would you describe your children's personalities?

How did you encourage a sense of independence in your children?

What do you hope your children will remember most about their childhood?

What values or principles do you hope to pass on to your children?

What traditions have you started with your own family?

What has helped you get through tough moments as a family?

What are some of your proudest moments as a parent?

What were your favourite
travel destinations after you turned 30?

How have you coped with any losses of family or loved ones?

How did you feel about turning 40?
What did you do to celebrate?

How did you go about making major decisions? Did you find them difficult or easy?

Was there a major change that happened in your life during this time, such as a new job, relationship or setback?

Which book or film has had the most impact on you as an adult?

Is there a movie, book, or TV show that you return to for comfort?

LATER LIFE

Which piece of clothing or object holds the most sentimental value to you and why?

What is the longest friendship you have had?

List all the places you have lived over the years.

What are your favourite memories from family gatherings or reunions?

How would your closest loved ones describe you?

If you could start your career over again, would you pursue the same one? Why or why not?

What are some of the most important values you hope to pass on to your grandchildren?

What advice would you give to young people?

What are three things you would tell young people not to worry about?

1.

2.

3.

How do you stay connected with your extended family?

What actions do you take to give back to
your community or support causes you care about?

What is on your bucket list?
Is there anything you hope to tick off soon?

What are the things that bring you the most joy?

What new hobbies or interests have you picked up recently?

How do you like to stay physically and mentally active?

What is your favourite way to spend a quiet day at home?

How do you like to spend your mornings?

If you could use a time machine and travel back to a particular year of your life which would you choose and why?

What are you most grateful for at this stage in your life?

Which books, TV shows, or movies have been your favourites in recent years?

Have your tastes in food, music or books changed in this stage of life?

How do you imagine the world your children will live in as they get older?

Are there things you notice now about people or places or nature, that you've never noticed before?

What beliefs do you hold about the afterlife and what happens to us when we die?

What are some of the most significant changes you've seen in society over your lifetime?

What historical events have had the most impact on you personally?

What is your proudest accomplishment and why?

What surprises you the most about the world today?

What do you want your legacy to be?

MEMENTOS